DKfindout! World War II

Author: Brian Williams
Consultant: Simon Adams

Penguin Random House

Senior editor Marie Greenwood
Senior designer Ann Cannings
US Editor Elizabeth Searcy
US Senior editor Shannon Beatty
Jacket coordinator Francesca Young
Jacket designer Amy Keast, Suzena Sengupta
Picture researcher Nishwan Rasool
Managing editor Laura Gilbert
Managing art editor Diane Peyton Jones
Pre-production producer Dragana Puvacic
Producer Isabell Schart
Art director Martin Wilson
Publisher Sarah Larter
Publishing director Sophie Mitchell
Educational consultant Jacqueline Harris

Designed, edited, and project-managed
for DK by Dynamo Ltd.

First American Edition, 2017
Published in the United States by DK Publishing
1450 Broadway, Suite 801, New York, NY 10018

Copyright © 2017 Dorling Kindersley Limited
DK, a Division of Penguin Random House LLC
19 20 21 10 9 8 7 6 5 4
007–299050–Sept/2017

DK books are available at special discounts when purchased in
bulk for sales promotions, premiums, fund-raising, or
educational use. For details, contact: DK Publishing Special
Markets, 1450 Broadway, New York, NY 10018 SpecialSales@dk.
com

Printed and bound in Malaysia

A WORLD OF IDEAS:
SEE ALL THERE IS TO KNOW

www.dk.com

Contents

4 What led to World War II?

6 Rise of the Nazis

8 The children escape

10 War begins

12 Key players

14 Living with the enemy

16 Operation Dynamo

18 Wartime women

20 Battle of Britain

22 Propaganda

24 Wartime entertainment

Winston Churchill

Canteen

German helmet

Fat Man bomb

26 Battles at sea

28 Animal heroes

30 Tanks into Russia

32 Airpower

34 The Holocaust

36 Anne Frank

38 Desert warfare

40 Growing up in the war

42 Pearl Harbor

44 Wartime food

46 Code breakers

48 D-day

50 City bombings

52 War ends in Europe

54 Atomic bomb

56 After the war

58 World War II facts and figures

60 Glossary

62 Index

64 Acknowledgments

Poppy

Spitfire

Wartime poster

Radio

Nazi eagle

What led to World War II?

1918 World War I ends
World War I lasted from 1914 to 1918. Most of the fighting was in Europe and the Middle East. It is also called the Great War.

Hitler's rise to power after World War I paved the way for the largest, deadliest war in history. World War II lasted six years, and fighting spread throughout Europe into Africa, Asia, and the Pacific Islands.

1935 New weapons
Germany becomes more powerful. The country begins making new weapons, including bomber planes.

1933 Hitler comes to power
The German people vote for the Nazi Party and Adolf Hitler. Hitler vows to make Germany strong again after its defeat in World War I.

German Dornier Do 17 bomber

German army helmet

1936 Germany on the move
After World War I, German armed forces were not allowed in the Rhineland, a German region that bordered France. In March 1936, German troops re-enter it.

German tanks
The Germans tested tanks in secret. They tried out their new Panzers, such as this PzKw II tank, in mock (pretend) battles.

1939 World War II begins
Europe had tried to avoid war by letting Hitler's army grow and take over other countries. This approach failed, because Hitler wanted more. In September 1939, Germany invades Poland.

1920s Money loses value
The world struggles after the war. The same amount of money buys less and less each day. The Germans, who had lost the war, suffer most.

Children playing with stacks of worthless German cash

Poppies
About 18 million people died in World War I. Today, people wear poppies to remember all those who have died in wars.

1930s No jobs, no money
The money crisis leads to banks closing all over the world. Factories close, too. Many people lose their jobs.

Jobless people marching in protest in England

Swastika
New leaders promised better times. Mussolini came to power in Italy. In Germany, Hitler made the swastika the flag of the new Nazi Party.

1937 Japan attacks China
China is weak because of civil (internal) war. In July, Japan invades, seeing the chance to lead Asia and make a new empire.

Rising sun flag of Japan

1938 Takeovers
Hitler makes Austria part of Germany. He also takes over part of Czechoslovakia (what is now the Czech Republic and Slovakia).

! WOW!
Germany had **no air force** after 1918. New pilots learned by **flying gliders.**

Rise of the Nazis

Difficult times followed World War I. Germany had lost the war and had to pay those who won. German money lost value, and banks were forced to shut. Factories closed down. People lost jobs and hope. They turned to the Nazis, led by Adolf Hitler, who promised to make Germany great.

Hitler

Hitler became Germany's leader in 1933. His National Socialist Party was also known as the Nazis. Hitler stopped paying war damages and promised the German people new factories and roads. He also formed a new army and air force. He talked about a new German empire, or "Reich."

RALLIES

The Nazis punished anyone who spoke against them. They held huge rallies (public meetings) to whip up support. Bands played, banners waved, and soldiers and children marched. Hitler roused the crowds with fiery speeches. He promised Germany would rule Europe.

Hitler's ideas

Hitler was born in Austria. He joined Germany's army in World War I and became leader of the Nazi Party in 1921. In 1924, he went to prison where he wrote *Mein Kampf* (My Struggle). His book blamed Jewish people and Communists for Germany's problems.

Nazi symbols

The Nazis put their symbols everywhere, on flags, uniforms, buildings, and even schools. Their signs included this eagle and the swastika, an ancient cross. The Nazis used these emblems to show everyone who ruled Germany. Just seeing these symbols made many people proud, but they scared others.

OLYMPICS

The 1936 Olympic Games took place in Berlin. The Nazis used the games to show off. Crowds cheered every German winner. However, the star of the games was US athlete Jesse Owens. He won three gold medals, and Hitler walked out. Why? Owens was an African American. His success went against the Nazis' racist ideas.

Kristallnacht

On November 9, 1938, Nazi gangs trashed Jewish shops and attacked and killed many Jewish people. Nazis painted messages of hate on walls and doors. They threw homemade bombs. They set shops on fire and smashed windows. Shattered glass covered the streets. It was called Kristallnacht, or the "Night of Glass."

Children bravely began life in a strange land.

The children escape

After 1933, Jewish people lived in danger under Nazi rule. Many Jewish families sent their children away for safety. About 10,000 child refugees escaped to Britain. British children were also seeking shelter, because war seemed ever closer. They left city homes for the countryside as evacuees.

Kindertransport

Kindertransport means "children's transport" in German. It was an escape plan for Jewish children to flee to Britain. They traveled by train and ship. Many were scared, not knowing what awaited them. They found new homes with British families. But many never saw their own families again.

Refugee children needed travel passes called visas. British helpers got these for them.

Fleeing to freedom

This map shows the long journeys made across Europe to Britain from countries where Jewish people feared for their lives.

Kindertransport refugee statue at Liverpool Street station in London

Children took their favorite toys with them.

Nicholas Winton in 1938, with one of the children he rescued.

Escape by train

Nicholas Winton was a British Jew who wanted to help Jewish people. He went to Czechoslovakia (today the Czech Republic and Slovakia) and met Jewish families who wanted their children sent to safety. He found new homes for the refugees and trains to take them there. The first train left one day before the Nazis arrived. The last left the day before Britain went to war. In total, 669 children safely reached Britain.

Evacuees

Some British children living in towns and cities left home too. Families were under threat of bomb or gas attacks, so the government said children should go to the country. More than a million evacuees packed their bags, and parents put them on buses and trains to the countryside.

Evacuees wore labels that showed their names, addresses, schools, and where they were going.

War begins

When Germany attacked Poland on September 1, 1939, France and Britain declared war on Germany two days later. By the spring of 1940, fighting had spread. Germany invaded Denmark and Norway. Then it attacked the Netherlands, Belgium, and France. The German army was in control.

● Poland invaded, September 1939

Hitler saluted his soldiers as they left to invade Poland. British reporter Clare Hollingworth was in Poland at the time. She heard guns in the night and called the British embassy to say war had begun.

British army gas mask

● Preparing for air raids, September 1939

People in Britain got ready for air raids. They hung blackout curtains over the windows to stop enemy pilots from seeing lights at night. Each person had a gas mask, in case poison gas bombs fell.

! WOW!

Every person in Britain had a **gas mask**. That's a total of **38 million masks!**

This map shows German advances up to the summer of 1940.

Dutch cities bombed, May 1940

After Rotterdam in the Netherlands was bombed, the Dutch government surrendered. Germany used a new way of fighting called *blitzkrieg*, meaning "lightning war." The Germans sent in bombers and tanks to create terror before ground troops arrived.

KEY:
German advances

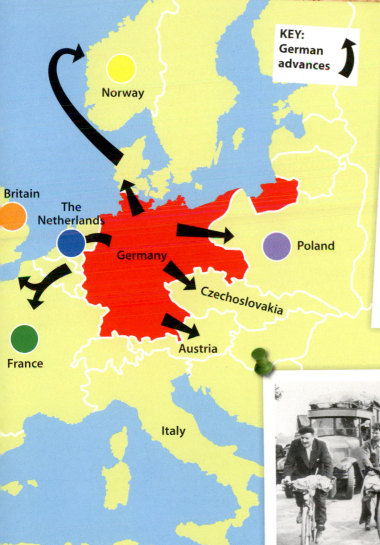

Norway

Britain

The Netherlands

Germany

Poland

Czechoslovakia

Austria

France

Italy

Norway invaded, June 1940

German troops took over Denmark, then Norway. Britain and France sent help, but Norway had to surrender in June 1940. German troops were in control.

Fall of France, June 1940

Germany invaded France in May 1940. Refugees (people escaping war) took all they could carry as they tried to get away. On June 22, 1940, France surrendered to Germany.

Key players

About 50 countries joined the war, as fighting spread from Europe to Asia and the Pacific. Some countries joined the Axis powers (with Germany). Others chose the Allies (with Britain, France, the United States, and the Soviet Union).

The Axis powers

Nazi Germany, with Adolf Hitler as leader, led the Axis side. Germany's main ally (partner) in Europe was Italy. Japan joined the Axis powers later, in 1941, when it attacked the United States.

GERMANY
Leader: ADOLF HITLER

Adolf Hitler (1889–1945) became the leader of Nazi Germany in 1933. He wanted revenge for Germany's defeat in World War I (1914–18). He held huge rallies and tried to turn people against Jews and Communists. He killed himself a week before Germany surrendered.

JAPAN
Leader: EMPEROR HIROHITO

Hirohito (1901–89) became Japan's emperor in 1926. He was against Japan's war plans in the 1930s but agreed to attack Pearl Harbor in 1941. In 1945 he took part in Japan's surrender and told his people to stop treating him as a god.

ITALY
Leader: BENITO MUSSOLINI

Benito Mussolini (1883–1945) became the leader of Fascist Italy in 1922. He wanted Italy to be a modern Roman Empire and became Hitler's ally to achieve this. In 1940 Italy joined the war but left the Axis powers in 1943. Mussolini was later caught and killed just before the war ended.

The Allies

Britain and France were allies. They went to war with Germany in 1939, after Germany attacked Poland. Other nations, including Australia, New Zealand, and Canada, joined the Allies. In 1941, the Soviet Union (Russia), the United States, and China joined as well.

UNITED STATES
Leader: FRANKLIN D. ROOSEVELT

Franklin D. Roosevelt (1882–1945) became president of the United States in 1933. He helped America recover from hard times in the 1930s. America joined the Allies in 1941, when Japan attacked Pearl Harbor. Roosevelt died just before the war ended.

GREAT BRITAIN
Leader: WINSTON CHURCHILL

Winston Churchill (1874–1965) became Britain's prime minister in 1940, when the country was already at war. Churchill's speeches inspired people to fight on. He worked closely with other Allied leaders, especially US president Roosevelt.

SOVIET UNION
Leader: JOSEPH STALIN

Joseph Stalin (1878–1953) became leader of the Soviet Union in1924. He got rid of all who stood in his way. Although Stalin and Hitler had agreed not to fight each other, in June 1941, Germany invaded Russia. The Russians fought back and defeated the Germans.

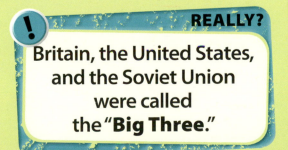

! REALLY?

Britain, the United States, and the Soviet Union were called the **"Big Three."**

Soldiers in Paris
German soldiers occupied Paris, the French capital, from June 1940 until August 1944. This group of German soldiers is walking by the Eiffel Tower.

Living with the enemy

By 1940, Hitler's armies had moved into much of Europe. People in Poland, Norway, the Netherlands, and most of France lived under German occupation. This meant they lived under enemy rule. People had to do what the Germans told them. But not everyone followed their rules, and some fought back in secret.

Fighting back

Secret groups of fighters called the French Resistance tried to stop Nazi rule. The Allies dropped weapons for them by parachute. They also sent in secret agents to help.

Secret messages
Resistance fighters sent secret messages using Morse code. Tapping keys on machines like this one sent coded information by radio.

Resistance fighters in Paris, 1944, helping overthrow German rule.

Street fighters
Men and women joined the Resistance. Some fought battles in the streets of towns and villages.

French hero
Jean Moulin (1899–1943) played a very important part in the Resistance. He used the code name Max. Moulin escaped to Britain but returned to France to help lead the Resistance. He was killed in 1943.

! WOW!

Lysander planes flew **secret agents** into and out of France. They often landed in fields.

R9125

Operation Dynamo

The German army invaded France in May 1940, pushing Allied soldiers out. Many gathered at a port on the northern coast of France called Dunkirk. The Germans closed in, trapping thousands of British and French men on the beaches. It seemed hopeless, but the Allies launched a mission called Operation Dynamo.

Pushed back to the English Channel, British and French troops faced defeat. Surprisingly, Hitler ordered the Germans to stop. This gave the Allies valuable time to plan an escape for the stranded men.

Britain sent all the ships it could, even small fishing boats. These "little ships," as they were called, sailed into shore to rescue the men.

The men at Dunkirk were out in the open, with nowhere to hide. They had to dig into the sand for shelter from German dive-bombers. Many soldiers were injured as the battle raged for days.

Troops were forced to leave their heavy guns and vehicles behind. Most had only rifles as they crowded onto the boats. German bombs and torpedoes made the sea crossing back to Britain very dangerous.

Soldiers waded out to the rescue boats. Big ships carried more men but had to wait farther from shore than the smaller craft.

The Dunkirk Medal was given to the soldiers at Dunkirk.

Operation Dynamo was expected to rescue around 35,000 troops. In just nine days, 900 ships saved 338,000 British and French soldiers.

Britain's prime minister Churchill called the rescue "a miracle."

Wartime women

Governments from many countries called on women to help with the war effort. Women took on many jobs that men usually did. They worked in factories and drove buses and fire trucks. They made planes, tanks, and other equipment. Some flew planes, cracked codes, or became secret agents. It changed the way women were viewed in the workplace forever.

Lettice Curtis

Expert pilot Lettice Curtis flew fighter and bomber planes. Along with other British women, she delivered new planes to air bases. Women pilots in the United States and Australia did the same jobs.

Land Army

To grow more food, people planted vegetables in parks and gardens. Women in Britain and the United States joined the Land Army to work on farms.

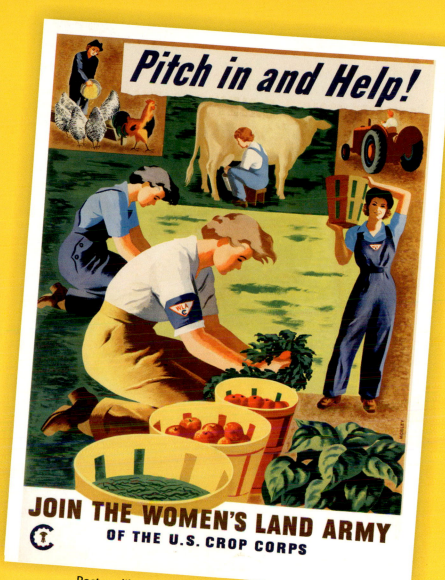

Posters, like this one from the USA, showed how women could help the war effort.

Women pilots of the Night Bomber Regiment

Soviet pilots

In the Soviet Union (Russia), women also fought in the war. This photograph shows a group of female pilots. Nicknamed Nachthexen (Night Witches) by the Nazis, these pilots dropped bombs in the dark. They turned off their engines and glided to their targets. The enemy did not hear them coming until the bombs fell.

Luftwaffe

The German air force, or Luftwaffe, sent 1,500 aircraft into battle. They flew from airfields in France and Norway. German pilots had fought air battles before. They were confident that they would win.

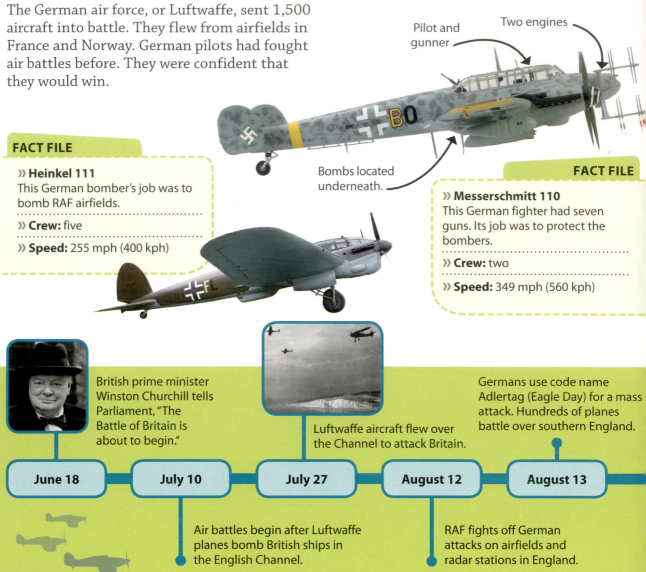

Pilot and gunner

Two engines

Bombs located underneath.

FACT FILE

» **Heinkel 111**
This German bomber's job was to bomb RAF airfields.

» **Crew:** five

» **Speed:** 255 mph (400 kph)

FACT FILE

» **Messerschmitt 110**
This German fighter had seven guns. Its job was to protect the bombers.

» **Crew:** two

» **Speed:** 349 mph (560 kph)

British prime minister Winston Churchill tells Parliament, "The Battle of Britain is about to begin."

Luftwaffe aircraft flew over the Channel to attack Britain.

Germans use code name Adlertag (Eagle Day) for a mass attack. Hundreds of planes battle over southern England.

June 18	July 10	July 27	August 12	August 13

Air battles begin after Luftwaffe planes bomb British ships in the English Channel.

RAF fights off German attacks on airfields and radar stations in England.

Battle of Britain

Hitler planned to invade Britain in June 1940. He knew he would have to destroy Britain's Royal Air Force (RAF) first. Only then could the German army cross the English Channel, safe from air attack. The fierce fighting between the German and British air forces was called the Battle of Britain.

Royal Air Force

Britain's RAF began the battle with about 500 fighter aircraft. Many pilots were young, but they learned quickly. Britain also had radar. Radar used sound waves to pick out enemy aircraft and show where they were.

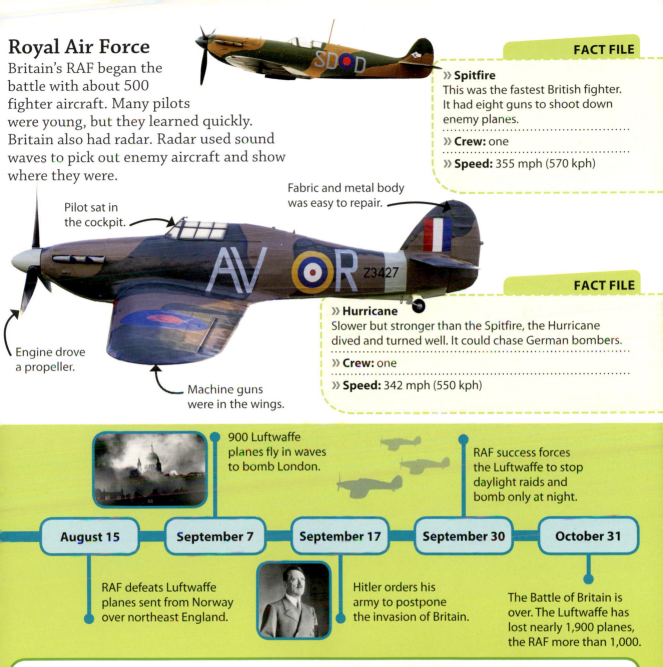

Pilot sat in the cockpit.

Fabric and metal body was easy to repair.

Engine drove a propeller.

Machine guns were in the wings.

FACT FILE

» **Spitfire**
This was the fastest British fighter. It had eight guns to shoot down enemy planes.

» **Crew:** one

» **Speed:** 355 mph (570 kph)

FACT FILE

» **Hurricane**
Slower but stronger than the Spitfire, the Hurricane dived and turned well. It could chase German bombers.

» **Crew:** one

» **Speed:** 342 mph (550 kph)

900 Luftwaffe planes fly in waves to bomb London.

RAF success forces the Luftwaffe to stop daylight raids and bomb only at night.

August 15	September 7	September 17	September 30	October 31

RAF defeats Luftwaffe planes sent from Norway over northeast England.

Hitler orders his army to postpone the invasion of Britain.

The Battle of Britain is over. The Luftwaffe has lost nearly 1,900 planes, the RAF more than 1,000.

Who won?

Throughout the summer of 1940, people on the ground watched battles in the sky, called dogfights. Bombs fell and planes crashed, but Hitler's army did not invade Britain. He told the Luftwaffe to bomb cities instead. The RAF had won the Battle of Britain. However, the war was not over yet.

This German Heinkel 111 was shot down and crashed in Essex.

Propaganda

Countries didn't use only weapons to fight the war. Propaganda is the use of words and pictures to get people to think in a certain way. Governments on both sides used propaganda to make people do things for their country. They tried to make the enemy look bad and keep their side thinking they could win, sometimes by lying to people with news that was false.

This poster from the United States shows a female factory worker. It was used to get people to "roll up their sleeves" and work hard.

Posters

Eye-catching posters were used for many purposes by both sides. People were encouraged to work hard, look out for spies, and waste nothing. Posters were displayed at school, work, and in the street.

This Nazi poster urges French people to switch sides and join the Germans. "You will win," the poster promises.

AVEC TES CAMARADES EUROPÉENS SOUS LE SIGNE ⚡⚡ TU VAINCRAS !

Radio

In the days before television, people got a lot of their news from the radio. War leaders used the radio to give rousing speeches. The enemy tried to spread fear with fake news, but it often seemed far-fetched and not believable.

American soldiers listening to news from back home.

Newspapers

Governments told newspapers what to print, to make sure no war secrets slipped out. When battles were won, the headlines and stories were big. When battles were lost, they were much smaller. Advertisements gave tips on keeping healthy and safe.

Cartoons like this one made fun of the enemy.

Film

People loved going to the movies. Before a film, newsreels (short films) showed victories in battle and people working hard for the war effort. Many films had war themes.

German director Leni Riefenstahl made films of Nazi rallies and the Berlin Olympics.

! WOW!

Allied planes dropped **6 billion propaganda leaflets** on Europe.

War savings

The war cost huge sums of money. Government posters asked people to buy war bonds. This was a way of helping the war effort and saving money at the same time.

ATTACK ATTACK ATTACK

BUY WAR BONDS

Children playing hospital with their dolls.

Toys
Children played with old, patched-up dolls, teddies, and bikes. Many toys had war themes. Most toys were made of wood. Metal and plastic were valuable and therefore rarer.

Playtime
Children copied what they saw and heard. They played hospital and air raid. They pretended to be fighter pilots zooming through the sky. They fought pretend fires, drove make-believe ambulances, or marched like soldiers.

Casablanca (1942), a wartime love story

Movies
People went to the movies to escape the worries of war and be entertained. They enjoyed romantic dramas, like the American film *Casablanca*.

Wartime entertainment

People all over the world had a lot to worry about in wartime. They needed cheering up, and entertainers did their part for the war effort. Radio, films, music, and sports all helped people to keep going. Children still played games, but new toys were a real treat.

Games

Many board games and playing cards had wartime themes. Some featured new characters, such as "warden" and "evacuee." Battle puzzles and "hunt-the-sub" games were also popular.

Evacuee card game was a wartime version of the game Happy Families.

Homemade wooden truck and plane

Radio

Families gathered around the radio (called a wireless) to listen to the news. They also enjoyed comedy, variety shows, and music. There were radio shows for children too, with stories, talks, and songs.

Entertaining the troops

Stars gave live shows for troops and factory workers. British singer Vera Lynn was famous for her wartime songs. "Lili Marlene" was a well-known song that was popular with both Allied and Axis audiences.

Vera Lynn singing to British troops in 1940.

Wartime radio

Battles at sea

Naval forces fought battles at sea, above and below the waves. Cargo ships traveled in groups (convoys) with food, oil, and other supplies. Warships cruised on the surface. Submarines moved beneath the waves, while aircraft flew overhead.

Acanthus

Small warships protected cargo ships and hunted submarines. They cleared away floating bombs, called mines. *Acanthus*, built in Britain, fought in Norway's navy.

Bismarck had eight big guns and 44 smaller guns. It also had two aircraft.

Hornet

The US Navy's *Hornet* was an aircraft carrier with 90 planes. It sank in 1942 in a battle in the Pacific Ocean.

Planes took off from the flat deck, or carrier. They landed on it, too.

Japanese I-400

This was the war's biggest submarine at 400 ft. (122 m) long. It had a crew of 144 and could carry aircraft, even underwater!

The submarine had to surface before a plane took off. A catapult sent the plane into the air to spy over the sea.

🇺🇸 Liberator

America's Liberator bombers flew far out over the Atlantic Ocean. They were used to hunt German submarines. When Liberators found a submarine, they attacked it with bombs.

🇩🇪 Condor

German pilots flew Condors on sea patrols. They hunted Allied ships, dropping bombs to sink them. Condors could fly nonstop for up to 14 hours.

Wings and engines were high up to keep clear of the water.

🇬🇧 Sunderland

These British flying boats could take off from and land on water. Each had a crew of 10, with eight guns, as well as bombs. They could fly 2,485 miles (4,000 km).

🇩🇪 *Bismarck*

The mighty *Bismarck* was one of the German navy's greatest battleships. British warships chased and sank it in 1941.

🇩🇪 German U-boat

Short for "undersea boats," U-boats were German submarines. They lay hidden underwater, ready to fire missiles at ships. Submarines used electric motors underwater and diesel motors on the surface.

The captain could look around using a periscope while the U-boat was hidden beneath the surface.

GI Joe
the pigeon

Trained pigeons carried messages tied to their legs. GI Joe once saved 100 Allied soldiers from being bombed by their own side by flying 20 miles (32 km) in 20 minutes. This gave the soldiers time to get away.

Upstart
the police horse

Upstart worked in London during air raids. Once, a bomb exploded nearby, and he was lucky to survive. Glass and metal flew through the air, but Upstart stayed calm. He led people to safety while more bombs fell.

Animal heroes

Did you know that animals went to war, too? Some even won medals, such as the Dickin Medal, for bravery. The first winners of this medal were three pigeons in 1943. They delivered urgent messages that saved many lives. Other animal heroes included dogs and horses. To be awarded a Dickin Medal took special courage.

The PDSA Dickin Medal

Rex the mine dog

Rex was a stray black labrador. Working with the British Army, like the dog pictured, his keen nose sniffed out land mines. Mines were small bombs, hidden just under the ground. Brave Rex saved many soldiers.

A ship's cat

Many ships kept a cat to keep disease-carrying rats away. Cats at sea lived through battles, storms, and even shipwrecks. When danger was over, most cats found a warm place to curl up and go to sleep.

5 ANIMAL HERO FACTS

1 **Judy the pointer dog** comforted people who were locked up in Japanese prison camps.

2 **Rip the stray dog** helped to find people hurt during the air raids on London in 1941.

3 **Sheila the collie** rescued four US airmen lost in the snow after a plane crash in Scotland.

4 **Regal the police horse** kept calm when his London stable was firebombed—twice.

5 **Rifleman Khan the German shepherd** saved a soldier from drowning during a battle in the Netherlands.

Tanks into Russia

In June 1941, German armies marched into Russia, which was then part of the Soviet Union. Hitler had broken his word not to attack the country. He sent three million men and 3,000 tanks into Russia, hoping for a quick victory. But Russia is a huge country, and its winters are freezing cold. The invasion turned into the most terrible battle of the war so far. The fighting in Russia lasted four years, until early 1945.

German PzKw III

Fast-moving German tanks traveled in groups. Each tank had a crew of five. This included a commander, a driver, a radio man, and two gunners. The commander gave orders by radio.

These containers held extra diesel fuel. The tank could go 93 miles (150 km) before it needed filling up.

The engine drove wheels that were inside metal tracks.

Battle for Stalingrad

In 1942, the Russian city of Stalingrad became a battlefield. When the winter came, the German army froze. Soldiers had little warm clothing, food, or fuel. Russian fighters trapped 250,000 Germans in the city. They surrendered in January 1943. In total, the battle cost more than one million lives on both sides, including Russian civilians.

Street fighting
This photo shows Russian troops fighting the Germans in Stalingrad. Russians were better prepared for the freezing conditions.

A rotating turret could swing the gun in a full circle.

The commander had the best view from the domed top, or cupola.

The main gun was powerful enough to blast holes in buildings.

The smaller machine gun was next to the tank's driver.

7

German stick grenade
After pulling a cord, a German soldier had only a few seconds to throw one of these bombs before it exploded.

Straw boots
Some German soldiers wore straw boots over their ordinary boots. They were trying to keep their feet warm and dry in the snow.

Harsh winters
People in Stalingrad suffered cold and hunger. Many died on both sides. The city lay in ruins.

Airpower

During World War II, people in factories worked hard to make bombers, fighters, and transport planes. New aircraft were bigger, better, and faster than ever before. The Allies' mighty airpower helped them win the war.

! WOW!

Only a Lancaster could carry a **Grand Slam** bomb, which was as heavy as two elephants!

Avro Lancaster

The Lancaster was the RAF's best bomber. Hundreds flew from Britain to bomb targets in Germany at night. The Lancaster had the same engine as the Spitfire.

FACT FILE

» **Speed:** 272 mph (438 kph)

» **Crew:** seven

» **Weapons:** eight machine guns in three turrets and 14,000 lb. (6,350 kg) of bombs

De Havilland Mosquito

Unlike most aircraft, Mosquitoes were made mostly of wood. They were very fast fighters or bombers. Mosquitoes also flew in front of Lancasters, dropping flares to light up targets.

FACT FILE

» **Speed:** 366 mph (589 kph)

» **Crew:** two

» **Weapons:** four cannons in nose, machine guns, bombs, and cameras for taking pictures of enemy targets

Douglas C-47 Skytrain

More than 10,000 of these US transport planes were built. C-47s carried troops, supplies, and wounded soldiers. They also flew secret agents into Nazi-occupied Europe.

FACT FILE

» **Speed:** 230 mph (370 kph)

» **Crew:** three

» **Weapons:** no guns, instead carried 6,000 lb. (2,722 kg) of cargo, 28 paratroopers, or 14 wounded soldiers

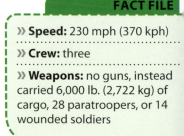

Tail fin showed the Nazi swastika.

Pilot sat in the cockpit.

Long nose helped make the aircraft streamlined.

Two turbojet engines sucked in air, forcing it out the rear.

Messerschmitt Me 262

The first jet warplane was Germany's Sturmvogel (Storm Bird). With no propellers, this jet was extremely fast, taking the Allies by surprise in 1944. However, jet planes came too late to save Germany.

FACT FILE

» **Speed:** 540 mph (870 kph)

» **Crew:** one

» **Weapons:** four guns in nose (carrying bombs slowed the jet down)

P-51 Mustang

The Mustang was America's best fighter plane. It was fast and could also fly far. Mustangs flew from Britain to Germany to defend Allied bombers from enemy fighters.

FACT FILE

» **Speed:** 437 mph (703 kph)

» **Crew:** one

» **Weapons:** six machine guns, plus rockets and bombs for attacking tanks, trains, and trucks

Kawasaki Ki-100

Japan's Ki-100 could fly very high, reaching heights of more than 33,000 ft. (10,000 m). It was rushed into action in 1945 to fight high-flying Allied bombers.

FACT FILE

» **Speed:** 367 mph (590 kph)

» **Crew:** one

» **Weapons:** four guns in fuselage (body) and wings, plus bombs or extra fuel tanks

The Holocaust

Hitler and the Nazis forced Jewish people to live in Jewish-only areas, called ghettos. The ghettos were shut off from outside help, and conditions were unbearable. People were also sent to camps. More than six million Jewish people, along with other groups of people who Hitler thought of as "undesirable," were killed. After the war, in 1945, the world learned of the Nazis' mass murders, called the Holocaust.

Yellow star

Nazis made Jewish people wear a yellow star on their clothes in the ghettos and in the camps. On it was the word Jude (Jew). Every camp prisoner had a number tattooed on their arm.

Auschwitz

The camps that the Nazis sent people to were called concentration camps. The biggest one was Auschwitz, in Poland. The Nazis killed more than one million people there. Trains carried men, women, and children to the camp every day.

Concentration camps

The camps were built throughout Europe. Here, people were forced to work. Along with Jews, the camps contained people who spoke out or fought against the Nazis. Many prisoners died from illness, hunger, and harsh treatment. Others were killed.

Map showing where the biggest camps were.

This is the gateway to Auschwitz. Today, people visit the site to remember the dead.

Remembering the Holocaust

Every year, Holocaust Memorial Day is held on January 27. People remember those who died. They mark this special day in the hope that nothing like the Holocaust ever happens again.

Holocaust memorial in Pennsylvania

Anne Frank

Anne Frank was a German Jewish girl. To escape the Nazis, her family fled to Amsterdam in the Netherlands. However, in 1940 the Nazis arrived in Amsterdam. Fearing for their lives, the family hid in two rooms behind an office wall. It was there that Anne wrote her diary.

Anne wrote her diary by hand in small notebooks. She added photographs to remind her of times gone by. In the entries below, Anne talks about her grandmother with great fondness.

Anne Frank aged 12, before she went into hiding.

Young writer

Anne was born in 1929. She loved to write and, on her 13th birthday, began keeping a diary. She wrote about growing up and how it felt to be shut away, hiding from the Nazis.

Nazi rule

Under Nazi rule, Jewish people in the Netherlands could not live normal lives. They had to wear yellow stars to single them out. They could not use public transportation or ride bikes. Jewish children weren't allowed to go to school. In 1942 the Frank family feared Anne's sister, Margot, would be sent to a work camp. The family hid above Mr. Frank's office.

Nazi soldiers march through a Dutch town in May 1940.

This photo shows Anne with her older sister, Margot. Her grandmother is in the background.

This photo shows Anne with Margot one year later.

Secret doorway into the Frank family's hiding place.

The secret hideout

Four people joined the Frank family in their two-room hiding place. One was an older boy, Peter, who became a friend. They could not go out, but friends brought food and news. Anne was in hiding from 1942 to 1944. Then Nazi police came and took them away. Anne died in Bergen-Belsen camp in 1945. She was 16 years old. Only her father survived the war.

Desert warfare

In 1940, war spread to North Africa. German and Italian armies faced British and Allied troops in the desert. With tanks, planes, and trucks, they fought in the heat and dust. The Allies' victory at El Alamein, Egypt, was a turning point in the war.

Pilots flew over the pyramids of Egypt. They watched for enemy tanks and trucks crossing the vast North African desert.

The Desert Rats

British soldiers called themselves the Desert Rats. The little animal on their flag is a jerboa, a rodent that lives in the desert.

Desert life

In the desert, daytime temperatures soared to more than 86°F (30°C), but nights turned cold. Soldiers wore hats to protect them from the sun and lightweight clothes, including shorts. Men slept in tents or trucks. Out on patrol, they carried extra water and gas in cans. Even canned food melted.

Desert cap
This German Afrika Korps cap had a flap to protect the neck from sunburn. Other hats had wide brims.

Arab headdress
Some Allied soldiers took to wearing local clothes that suited desert conditions. This Arab headdress kept a soldier's head cool by day. It gave extra warmth at night.

Water bottle
Every soldier needed a canteen, or water bottle. The desert had few oases (natural wells). If a soldier ran out of water, he could die.

Growing up in the war

War changed children's lives, too. Fathers left home and went to fight. Mothers went out to work. Children wondered if life would ever be the same again. Rationing meant less food to eat. There were safety drills at school. During air raids, children slept in cold, damp shelters. Even once they had grown up, people who were children in wartime never forgot the hardship and danger they faced.

Gas mask
Colorful masks like this one were given to toddlers to make them more fun to wear.

Working hard

Teachers in Japan told children that they must work for their emperor. Children worked on farms, as well as in factories. Even common food, such as rice, was rationed. It was hard to work when hungry. Radio news told people Japan was winning to keep their spirits up.

Hitler Youth

In Germany, Hitler wanted children to grow up as Nazis. Schools taught Nazi ideas, and children were encouraged to join Nazi youth groups. Beginning at age 10, boys joined the Hitler Youth. Girls belonged to the League of German Girls. Children learned to follow orders, so that they would be ready to fight.

Farm work

In Britain, children were evacuated from towns and cities to keep them safe from bombs. They went to live in the countryside, and many worked on farms. They learned to milk cows and grow vegetables. Enemy prisoners of war were also sent to work on farms. Children often made friends with them.

Collecting junk

During the war, it was important not to waste anything. Americans were asked to collect junk, and children helped with this. They saved toothpaste tubes for metal and rubber bands for tires. Old stockings could be recycled to make parachutes for the war.

Making weapons
Weapons factories had few men, so women and children worked there. Children did factory work after school, making parts for planes and guns.

Uniforms
Like soldiers, German children received uniforms from the Nazis. Children marched in bands, camped, and kept in shape. Most joined the youth groups. It was safer to be like everybody else.

Dig for victory
Food was in short supply. Children dug "victory gardens" at school, home, and in public parks. They grew vegetables, fruit, and herbs. Others, like the children in this photograph, helped with the harvest.

Anything goes
American children hunted for scrap metal, such as tin cans or old stoves, as in this picture. The metal was melted down and used again to make tanks, ships, and planes.

Pearl Harbor

On December 7, 1941, hundreds of Japanese planes flew over Pearl Harbor, the US naval base in Hawaii. With no warning, the planes attacked the base, which held almost 100 warships. They left ships on fire or sinking. It angered Americans and pushed them to join the war.

Pearl Harbor on fire
Ships were blown up and many sank. Hundreds of people onboard ships died. Rescuers fought to put out fires and save lives.

3 PEARL HARBOR FACTS

1 **The 360 Japanese planes** hit all eight battleships in the port. Later, six ships went back into action.

2 **More than 2,000 people** were killed in the attack. More than 1,000 were hurt.

3 **Japan had 33 ships** north of Hawaii. Their pilots flew from six aircraft carriers. They lost 29 planes in the attack.

Nakajima torpedo bomber
Japanese bomber pilots dropped torpedoes into the sea. The missiles sped underwater to their targets, then exploded.

Japanese pilot's helmet
Japan's navy was proud of its carrier pilots. They went home as heroes.

USS *Arizona*

The US battleship *Arizona* blew up and sank during the attack on Pearl Harbor. The wreck is now the final resting place for 1,000 crew members who lost their lives. A memorial stands above it, listing the names of those killed.

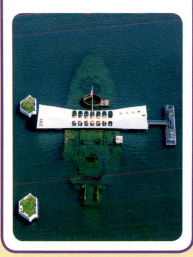

Weekly rations

Everywhere food was rationed. Even babies had ration books. Children got more milk and eggs than grown-ups but less of everything else. Babies got free orange juice, too.

Ration book
Everyone was given a ration book to show at each store they went to. They handed over coupons and money to buy their rations.

Checked off
The book listed which foods you could buy. Shopkeepers checked off each week's coupon.

Sugar
Many people stopped adding sugar to tea or coffee. Foods containing sugar, such as jam, cake, and other desserts, became rare treats.

Tea and coffee
Tea and coffee were rationed. American cafés had a "one-cup" rule for coffee. British people might save leftover tea leaves to make the next pot.

Meat
The best meat went to the army or the navy. In most countries everyone else had to get by on much less. Spam, a type of canned meat, came over from the United States in 1941 to help feed hungry Britons.

Wartime food

The war threatened food supplies. Cargo ships were now needed to carry weapons, so food from overseas vanished from supermarkets. Fighting destroyed farms and food stores. Farmers worked harder, and governments in many countries introduced rationing. This limited how much food people could buy, giving everyone a fair share.

Bread
Starting at the end of 1942, German people were allowed only half a loaf of bread a day. Germans ate black rye bread, often mixed with "wood flour" (sawdust).

Grow your own
Vegetables were also hard to get hold of, so more people grew their own vegetables in the garden. Flower beds in parks were dug up and used to grow potatoes and cabbages.

Dig for Victory
This poster urged everyone to grow their own vegetables.

Your own vegetables all the year round...
if you
DIG FOR VICTORY NOW

Milk
Milk was rationed, and people used canned or powdered milk when they ran short.

Eggs
Britons were allowed to buy only one egg a week, so many people kept hens for eggs. The United States sent cans of dried eggs to Europe. Dried eggs kept for months. They were used in baking or to make omelettes.

Butter
A package of butter had to last two weeks in both Britain and Germany. Leftover fats could be collected and turned into explosives.

Rice
In Japan, evacuee children from towns had to work in rice fields. Still, many families went hungry. In India, there was a terrible famine in 1943 when rice stocks ran out.

7 WAR FOOD FACTS

Food and drink

1 **Carrolade** was a drink made from carrot and rutabaga juice. People also made carrot jam.

2 **In Japan**, dinner might be a fish and two vegetable leaves.

3 **In Britain,** sweets were rationed from 1942 until 1953, long after the war had ended.

4 **Germans** drank fake coffee made from acorns. Americans drank coffee with chicory and other foods added.

5 **By 1944,** many Dutch people were starving. Some people were so hungry they ate tulip bulbs.

6 **The Tower of London's** moat was dug up and used for a vegetable garden.

7 **Snoek,** a type of fish from South Africa, was shipped over to Britain in cans, because local fish were not being caught. But people hated it! After the war, cans of snoek went on sale as cat food.

WOW!
People in Europe missed fruits grown overseas, such as **bananas**, which were rare.

Code breaking

In war, both sides want to keep their plans secret. They send messages in code, using mixed-up words, letters, and numbers. To read them, people must unlock the code. Both sides used machines that could do this quickly. The Allies won because they "cracked" the Axis codes first.

German Enigma machine

Enigma

German code machines were called Enigma, meaning "a puzzle." Polish scientists found out how it worked. They made a copy and showed it to Britain. By 1940, the British code breakers could understand most German secret radio messages.

! WOW!

Code breakers' jobs were **top secret**. They didn't tell anyone what they were doing.

Code breakers were good at science, math, and puzzles.

Station X

Station X was Bletchley Park, a mansion in the countryside north of London. Here, more than 10,000 British code breakers set to work. They read German radio messages and figured out codes, such as Enigma's.

Bombe

German codes changed every day. To keep up, a brilliant math expert, along with other code breakers at Bletchley, made a machine named the Bombe. Its spinning wheels, or rotors, could break the new code each day.

Spinning wheels
Bombe's spinning rotors could run the same codes as multiple Enigma machines at once.

Colossus

The Germans also had an even better code machine called Lorenz. The Bletchley code breakers cracked it, but it was slow work, so they made the world's first electronic computer, called Colossus, to help. Colossus processed 5,000 letters and numbers every second. Its data helped the Allies plan the D-day landings in June 1944.

The team at Bletchley Park built Colossus for the code breakers.

Secret radio

Spies and agents on both sides used secret codes. They sent messages in Morse code by radio. They often hid the radio set in a suitcase that they could carry around.

Suitcase spy radio

D-day

After five years of war, Germany ruled most of Europe. The Allies were now ready to free France. They carefully planned an attack and trained troops for months. On June 6, 1944, the Allies landed in Normandy, France. This was D-day. By August 25, the Allies had freed Paris from Nazi rule. Within nine months, the war in Europe was over.

Allied soldiers reached the shore in landing craft. They ran down ramps into the water and waded ashore. Other landing craft carried tanks and trucks.

3 AMAZING FACTS

Normandy invasion

1. **More than 150,000 Allied soldiers** crossed the English Channel for the attack. Around 2,500 men died in the battle.

2. **Nearly 7,000 seacraft** were used in the invasion, including battleships and minesweepers.

3. **Allied planes flew 14,000** sorties (air missions) during the attack.

Duck boat

The US DUKW was a boat with wheels. On land it became a truck. It helped Allied troops land safely on D-day.

Sainte-Mère-Eglise · Utah · Omaha · Gold · Juno · Sword · Carentan · Bayeux · Caen

This map shows where soldiers from the United States, Britain, Canada, and France landed. Each beach had a code name.

City bombings

Air raids brought the war into people's homes. When warning sirens wailed, everyone took shelter. Bombs started fires and flattened buildings. Rescue teams helped people escape from bombed homes. Then everyone tried to repair the damage and carry on. Europe's worst city bombing happened in 1945, when Allied planes bombed the German city of Dresden.

Whistle
Hearing the warden's whistle meant "Take cover! Air raid!"

Helmet
A helmet protected the warden from broken glass, metal, wood, and bricks.

Firebomb
Blazes were started with dangerous firebombs. Throwing sand or water on a firebomb could put it out.

Identity card
Everyone carried an identity card, showing the owner's name, age, address, and other details.

Air-raid wardens
It was the job of air-raid wardens to keep people safe during air raids. They made sure lights were out during blackouts and helped people find shelters.

More than 1,000 Allied planes attacked Dresden. Bombs and fires destroyed its buildings. Many thousands of people died. Today, many buildings have been rebuilt to look just as they did before.

War ends in Europe

After D-day, the Allies knew they could win the war. They had more soldiers, tanks, and aircraft than Germany. In western Europe, the Americans, British, and other Allies freed France, Belgium, and the Netherlands. The Russians moved in from the east, freeing Poland. By April 1945, they had reached Berlin. On May 8, 1945, the war in Europe was over.

This map shows how the Allies attacked from 1943 to 1945, moving toward Germany.

KEY:
Allied
attacks

Britain

France

North Afri

Secret weapons

Germany had secret weapons, such as V-1s, which were flying bombs. V-2s, like this one, were supersonic rockets. However, they came too late to change the war.

The French celebrate their freedom in 1944.

● Paris free

French troops fought alongside the Allied army. On August 25, 1944, crowds cheered as French troops drove into Paris. The Germans had left. Soon afterward, all of France was free.

● Battle of the Bulge

Bad weather in December 1944 stopped Allied planes from flying. German soldiers attacked in Belgium. They pushed into the Allied line, making a "bulge." Then Allied bombers got back in the air. The German attack in the west fizzled out.

Russian Katyusha rocket launcher

🔴 Red rockets

Russia's Red Army fought across Poland and into Germany. Russian tanks, planes, and rockets destroyed German towns and villages. Many people fled west before the Red Army arrived.

USSR

Poland

Germany

Italy

🟣 German surrender

Russians were fighting in Berlin by January 1945. Some Nazis still hoped for peace, but others fought on. On April 30, Hitler killed himself in his bunker (underground base). The German army surrendered days later.

THE STARS AND STRIPES

EXTRA   EXTRA

HITLER DEAD

Fuehrer Fell at CP, German Radio Says; Doenitz at Helm, Vows War Will Continue

Churchill Hints Peace Is at Hand

US tank in the Battle of the Bulge

VE Day

People celebrated Victory in Europe Day (VE Day) on May 8, 1945. They danced, sang, and cheered. People waved flags and had parties in the street. They also remembered. Six long years of war had left many homeless, hurt, or dead.

1

Albert Einstein
The great German scientist Albert Einstein (1879–1955) knew the power of atomic energy. In 1939, he warned about the terrifying threat of the atom bomb. If the Nazis made it first, the Allies would lose the war.

2

3

Manhattan Project
Allied scientists began working at Los Alamos, New Mexico, in 1942. Nobody outside knew about the secret Manhattan Project. The project was to make the first atom bomb.

Fat Man
The atom bomb was first tested in the New Mexican desert in July 1945. The Allies made two war bombs, code-named Little Boy and Fat Man.

Atomic bomb

The Allies used a terrible new weapon in August 1945. Just one atomic bomb was powerful enough to destroy a whole city. After two of these bombs were dropped on Japan, the fighting stopped. World War II was now over.

4

Enola Gay
On August 6, 1945, the B-29 bomber *Enola Gay* dropped Little Boy on Hiroshima, Japan. Three days later, Fat Man exploded on Nagasaki, Japan.

5

Aftermath
The city of Hiroshima was in ruins after the atomic bomb. The city of Nagasaki was also destroyed. More than 240,000 people died because of the bombings. Japan surrendered on August 15, 1945.

The power of atoms

Everything in the universe is made of atoms. Scientists had been working to find out how atoms produce energy. In 1942, a team in Chicago built the first atomic reactor. This machine split atoms, releasing energy. The energy could have peaceful uses, including electricity. It could also make atom bombs.

Fermi's team
Born in Italy, Enrico Fermi was a scientist working in the United States. He led a team that showed how to control atomic power for human use.

Hiroshima today
This ruined building in Hiroshima stands as a peace memorial. It reminds people how precious peace is. It became a UNESCO World Heritage Site in 1996.

After the war

The war changed the world. The United States and the Soviet Union (Russia) were now the most powerful nations. These wartime allies soon became less friendly. Former enemies became partners. And war-damaged countries rebuilt towns and cities. People looked toward a better and peaceful future.

Coming home

Service members looked forward to their welcome home. People were also sad, remembering friends and family they had lost in the war.

School's back

Children sent to the country for their safety came home. Work began to rebuild schools damaged by bombing. Children helped put classrooms back in order. Normal work and play began again.

Rebuilding

In Britain, one home in every three was damaged. People needed new places to live, but rebuilding took time. Factories made prefabricated homes that could be built quickly and were put together like furniture.

War crimes

The Allies put Nazi leaders on trial for war crimes. The trials were held in Nuremberg, Germany. Leaders in Japan also faced punishment for their actions.

The Berlin Wall

The war ended with Germany and its capital, Berlin, split into two. Beginning in 1961, a wall divided the city. When the wall fell in 1989, Germany became one nation again.

The Cold War

After the war, some of the Allies became rivals. The Soviet Union (Russia) became locked in a power struggle with the United States and other Western countries. Each side wanted to show it had the best weapons. The Cold War, as it became known, lasted until 1991.

United Nations

In 1945, 51 countries founded an organization called the United Nations (UN). The UN works to help countries talk to each other and keep peace. There have been many wars since 1945, but no world war.

World War II facts and figures

Almost everything about World War II was newer, bigger, or different than before. Here are just a few facts about the biggest war in history.

During London air raids,

many families slept on underground railway platforms.

Many people felt safer underground.

2 is the number of days a week Germans were allowed hot water for washing (they had to save fuel).

The German V-2 rocket

flew so fast no one could hear it coming.

60,000,000

is the number of people believed to have died in World War II. This is more than in any other war.

US Marine Corps War Memorial

More than 100

British female pilots flew RAF planes from factories to airfields.

14

was the age of some German boy soldiers in the final battles against the Allies.

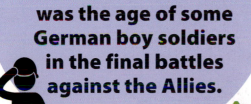
TICKET
ADMIT ONE
0783654 B

In movie theaters, when an air raid began, a message on screen told people they could leave if they liked. Then the film continued playing.

Australians, like the British, planted victory gardens to grow more food.

50 vs 9

50 Nations fought on the Allied side and 9 on the Axis side.

1,500,000

is the number of parts needed to build a Liberator bomber.

Glossary

Some words in the book may be new to you. This is what they mean. They will help you learn about World War II.

aircraft carrier Huge ship with warplanes that fly to and from its flat deck

air raid Attack from the sky, by planes dropping bombs

Allies People who join in a shared aim. The main Allies in World War II were Britain, the United States, France, and the Soviet Union (USSR)

atomic bomb Weapon using the power of split atoms to produce energy that destroys. Now called a nuclear weapon

Axis powers Nations on Germany's side in World War II, including Italy and Japan

battleship Large fighting ship, with big guns

blackout Ban on using lights in buildings at night so bombers couldn't spot them. People used thick curtains to hide light

Blitz Sudden, fast, and forceful air attack. From the German word *blitzkrieg*, meaning "lightning war"

code Way to keep a message secret by changing what it says. Knowing the code means someone can read it

Cold War The war without direct armed conflict that existed between the Soviet Union and the United States following World War II

communism Way of life in which everything belongs to the state, or government. The wealth and products of the state are divided between its citizens, or people

People carried gas masks, in case there was a gas attack.

concentration camp Place where people, mainly Jews, were kept prisoner in terrible conditions because of who they were. People in Nazi camps were used as slaves or killed

convoy Group of ships sailing together for safety

dogfight Close-range battle between two aircraft

empire Group of countries conquered and then ruled over by one nation

evacuee Person moved from danger to a safer place, often from the city to the countryside

fascism Political movement that started in Italy. Fascists oppose communism and believe in their nation above all others. The Nazis in Germany were fascists

fighter plane Fast plane armed with guns

gas mask Goggle-like mask worn over the nose and mouth to protect people from breathing in poison gas

ghetto City area in which the Nazis forced Jews to live

grenade Small bomb thrown by a soldier

Holocaust The mass killing of six million Jews, along with other groups of people, by the Nazis in World War II

invasion Going into an enemy's land by force

Jew Person whose own religion, or family religion, is Judaism

Kindertransport Train and ship journeys set up for some Jewish children to escape from the Nazis

landing craft Smaller boats used to take troops from big ships into shore

Luftwaffe Name of the German airforce

Morse code Code using dots and dashes for letters. Can be sent by flashing lights, flags, or long and short sounds

Nazi Member, or follower, of the Nazi Party (National Socialists) in Germany, led by Adolf Hitler

periscope Tube with mirrors that lets a submarine captain see what is above the water

propaganda Method used to change and control how people think and behave

propeller Spinning blades on an aircraft engine that move the plane

racism Thinking and acting against people of a different race because you believe you are better than they are

radar Bouncing radio waves off an object to reveal where it is. Used to locate enemy aircraft and ships

rallies Huge meetings to get people excited. The Nazis used rallies to spread support in the 1930s

rationing Fixed amount of food and supplies. Used to ensure supplies are shared

refugee Person leaving home and going to another country to escape danger

Resistance Secret army working against Nazi occupiers in France and other countries

siren Machine that makes a loud wailing sound to warn of a likely air raid

Soviet Union (USSR) Union of Soviet Socialist Republics, a Russian-led communist group of countries that fought on the Allied side in the war

German tank

spy Person who gathers information in secret. In war, each side uses spies to find out the other's secrets

submarine Boat that can sail on the sea or dive to travel deep underwater

swastika Nazi sign or symbol, taken from an ancient cross with bent arms. In the past, it was a symbol of the sun and good luck

torpedo Weapon fired from a submarine. It travels underwater, hits a target, and explodes

torture Causing people pain so that they will tell any secrets they know

U-boat German submarine

USSR See Soviet Union

war crime Action that breaks the laws or customs of warfare. Taking war criminals to court was new after World War II

Index

A

Afrika Korps 39
air-raid wardens 50
air raids 10, 28, 29, 40, 50–51, 58
aircraft carriers 26
Allied powers 12, 13, 59
animals in war 28–29
atomic bomb 54–55
Auschwitz 34–35
Australia 13, 59
Axis powers 12, 59

B

B-29 bomber 55
Battle of Britain 20–21
Battle of the Bulge 52
Battle of Stalingrad 30–31
battleships 26–27, 43
Berlin Olympic Games 7, 23
Berlin Wall 57
Bismarck 26–27
blitzkrieg 11
bomber planes 4, 11, 20, 27, 32, 43, 59
boy soldiers 59
Britain 8, 9, 10, 13, 16–17, 28, 29, 44–45, 46–47, 56, 58

C

Canada 13
children 8–9, 24–25, 40, 41, 44, 45, 59
China 5, 13
Churchill, Winston 13, 17, 20

code breaking 46–47
Cold War 57
Colossus computer 47
concentration camps 34–35, 37
Condor bomber 27
Czechoslovakia 5, 9

D

D-day landings 47, 48–49
death toll 58
desert warfare 38–39
Dornier Do 17 bomber 4
Douglas C-47 Skytrain 32
Dresden 50–51
DUKW amphibious vehicle 49
Dunkirk evacuation 16–17

E

Einstein, Albert 54
Enigma code machine 46
entertainment 23, 24–25
evacuees 8, 9, 40

F

farming 19, 40, 44, 45
Fermi, Enrico 55
fighter planes 20, 21, 32, 33
firebombs 50
flying boats 27
food supplies 19, 26, 40, 41, 44–45
France 11, 13, 14–15, 48–49, 52
Frank, Anne 36–37
French Resistance 15

G

gas masks 10, 40
German invasion 4, 10, 11, 13, 14–15, 30–31
Germany 4, 11, 12, 13, 14–15, 30–31, 40, 41, 45, 46, 47, 50–51, 53, 58
grenades 31

H

Heinkel 111 bomber 20, 21
Hirohito, Emperor 12
Hiroshima 55
Hitler, Adolf 4, 5, 6, 10, 12, 16, 20, 21, 34, 40, 52, 53
Hitler Youth 40, 41
Holocaust 34–35
home front 18–19, 40–41, 44–45, 58
Hurricane fighter 21

I

Italy 5, 12

J

Japan 5, 12, 13, 26, 40, 42–43, 45, 55, 57
Jewish people 6, 7, 8–9, 34–37

K

Kawasaki Ki-100 fighter 33
Kindertransport 8–9
Kristallnacht 7

L

Lancaster bomber 32
Land Army 19

Liberator bomber 27, 59
Lorenz code machine 47
Luftwaffe 20, 21
Lynn, Vera 25
Lysander aircraft 15

M
Manhattan Project 54
medals 17, 28
Mein Kampf 6
memorials 35, 43, 55, 58
messenger pigeons 28, 29
Messerschmitt 110 20
Messerschmitt Me 262 33
mines 26, 28
Morse code 15, 47
Mosquito fighter/bomber 32
Moulin, Jean 15
movies 23, 24, 59
Mussolini, Benito 5, 12

N
Nachthexen (Night Witches) 19
Nagasaki 55
naval warfare 26–27
Nazis 5, 6–7, 22, 34, 35, 36, 37, 40-41, 57
Netherlands 11, 14, 36–37, 45, 52
New Zealand 13
newspapers 23
Night Witches 19
Normandy landings 48–49
North Africa 38–39

Norway 11, 14, 26
Nuremberg trials 57

O
Operation Dynamo 16–17
outbreak of war 10–11
Owens, Jesse 7

P
P-51 Mustang fighter 33
Panzer tank 4, 30–31
Pearl Harbor 12, 13, 42–43
pilots 19, 59
planes 4, 11, 20–21, 27, 32–33, 43, 59
Poland 4, 10, 14, 34
poppies 5
postwar world 56–57
prefabricated homes 56
prisoners of war 40
propaganda 22–23

R
radar 21
radio 23, 25
rationing 40, 44–45
Red Army 53
refugees 8–9, 11
Roosevelt, Franklin D. 13
Royal Air Force (RAF) 20, 21
Russia 13, 30–31

S
secret agents 15, 32, 47
Soviet Union (Russia) 13, 19, 30–31, 53, 56, 57
Spitfire fighter 21

Stalin, Joseph 13
Stalingrad 30–31
Station X (Bletchley Park) 46–47
submarines 26, 27
Sunderland flying boat 27

T
tanks 4, 11, 30–31, 53
torpedoes 17, 43
toys and games 24–25
transport planes 32
Turing, Alan 47

U
U-boats 27
United Nations (UN) 57
United States 12, 13, 19, 22, 26, 32, 33, 42–43, 45, 56, 57

V
V-1 flying bombs 52
V-2 rockets 52, 58
VE Day 53

W
war crimes 57
war work 18–19, 40, 41
warships 26, 27
Winton, Nicholas 9
women 18–19, 41, 59
World War I 4, 5, 6, 12
World War II 4–5, 10-11, 52–53, 58

Acknowledgments

The publisher would like to thank the following people for their assistance in the preparation of this book: Brenda Williams (text consultant), Romi Chakraborty, Rashika Kachroo, and Jaileen Kaur (design), Vijay Kandwal and Dheeraj Singh (DTP).

The publisher would like to thank the following for their kind permission to reproduce their photographs:

(Key: a-above; b-below/bottom; c-centre; f-far; l-left; r-right; t-top)

1 **Dorling Kindersley:** Royal Airforce Museum, London (c). **2 Alamy Stock Photo:** Chronicle (bc/winston). **Dorling Kindersley:** Bradbury Science Museum, Los Alamos (crb); Wardrobe Museum, Salisbury (bl, bc). **2-3 Dorling Kindersley:** RAF Museum, Cosford (b). **3 123RF. com:** Scott Fensome / zollster (clb). **Alamy Stock Photo:** INTERFOTO (crb); World History Archive (cb). **Dorling Kindersley:** Wardrobe Museum, Salisbury (br). **4 Dorling Kindersley:** Gatwick Aviation Museum (cl); Wardrobe Museum, Salisbury (cr). **4-5 Dorling Kindersley:** The Tank Museum (b). **5 123RF.com:** Scott Fensome / zollster (tl). **Getty Images:** Keystone (cr); Universal Images Group (tr). **6 Getty Images:** Bettmann (cra); Topical Press Agency (bl); CARL DE SOUZA (crb). **7 Dorling Kindersley:** Wardrobe Museum, Salisbury (tr). **Rex Shutterstock:** AP (bl); The Weiner Library (br). **8 Alamy Stock Photo:** Heritage Image Partnership Ltd (br). **9 Alamy Stock Photo:** Ian Macpherson London (cra). **Getty Images:** Daily Herald Archive (crb). **iStockphoto. com:** Helen_Field (tr). **TopFoto.co.uk:** PA Photos (cl). **10 Dorling Kindersley:** Wardrobe Museum, Salisbury (cl). **Getty Images:** Hulton Archive (cra). **Rex Shutterstock:** Robert Kradin / AP (crb). **10-11 123RF.com:** Andreahast (background). **11 Alamy Stock Photo:** Prisma by Dukas Presseagentur GmbH (cra). **Getty Images:** Hulton Archive (bc); ullstein bild (cr). **12 Alamy Stock Photo:** David Cole (cr); Pictorial Press Ltd (crb). **Getty Images:** AFP (clb). **12-13 Dreamstime.com:** Gary Blakeley (c/ Flags). **13 Alamy Stock Photo:** Chronicle (cla); INTERFOTO (crb). **Getty Images:** Stock Montage (cra). **14-15 Dorling Kindersley:** Royal Airforce Museum, London (bc). **Getty Images:** Keystone-France (t). **15 Bridgeman Images:** Everett Collection (cr). **Dorling Kindersley:** The University of Aberdeen (cra). **Getty Images:** Keystone (br). **16 Getty Images:** (cr); Grierson (clb); Popperfoto (br). **17 Alamy Stock Photo:** Everett Collection Historical (crb). **Dorling Kindersley:** Wardrobe Museum, Salisbury (br). **Getty Images:** Hulton Archive (cra); Popperfoto (tl); IWM (clb). **18 Getty Images:** Hulton Deutsch. **19 Alamy Stock Photo:** World History Archive (tr). **Getty Images:** SVF2 (bl). **Rex Shutterstock:** (cla). **20 Alamy Stock Photo:** David Cole (cl). **Dorling Kindersley:** Flugausstellung (cra); Gatwick Aviation Museum (cra). **Getty Images:** ullstein bild (c). **21 Dorling Kindersley:** RAF Museum, Cosford (tc); Royal Airforce Museum, London (ca). **Getty Images:** Albert Harlingue (cb); Historical (cr); Planet News Archive (crb). **22 Getty Images:** John Parrot / Stocktrek Images (cra); Print Collector (clb). **23 Getty Images:** Bettmann (tl); Universal History Archive (ca); Historical (clb); David Pollack (br). **24 Alamy Stock Photo:** Glasshouse Images (crb). **Getty Images:** Reg Speller (tl). **24-25 V&A Images / Victoria and Albert Museum, London:** Museum of Childhood (c). **25 Alamy Stock Photo:** INTERFOTO (crb); Trinity Mirror / Mirrorpix (bl). **World of Playing Cards - www. wopc.co.uk:** Rex Pitts (tl, cra). **26 Dorling Kindersley:** Model Exhibition, Telford (cla); Scale Model World, Allan Toyne (b). **iStockphoto.com:** Hermsdorf (cb/flag); Suresh sharma (cb). **26-27 Dorling Kindersley:** Fleet Air Arm Museum (c); Gatwick Aviation Museum (t). **27 Dorling Kindersley:** Fleet Air Arm Museum, Richard Stewart (cb); Gatwick Aviation Museum (ca, cra/sunderland); Scale Model World, Jeremy Thomson (br). **iStockphoto.com:** Suresh sharma (cla); Sigurcamp (tl, c, clb); Tinnakorn (cra). **28 Alamy Stock Photo:** Lordprice Collection (tr). **bnps. co.uk:** Laura Jones (br). **Getty Images:** Hulton Archive (tl). **29 Alamy Stock Photo:** Atomic (clb); War Archive (tc). **30-31 Dorling Kindersley:** The Tank Museum (t). **Getty Images:** Sovfoto (b). **31 Dorling Kindersley:** 5te. Kompagnie Infanterie Regiment nr.28 'Von Goeben' (clb). **Getty Images:** Sovfoto (cb). **Imperial War Museum:** IWM (UNI 12917) (crb). **32 Dorling Kindersley:** Tony Agar (crb); RAF Battle of Britain Memorial Flight (cla); Gatwick Aviation (bl). **iStockphoto.com:** Tinnakorn (cra, cl, crb/flag). **33 Dorling Kindersley:** RAF Cosford (bl); Royal Airforce Museum, London (t). **Dorling Kindersley:** Gary Ombler / The Shuttleworth Collection **iStockphoto. com:** Hermsdorf (crb/japan); Tinnakorn (cl); Sigurcamp (cra). **34-35 Getty Images:** Scott Barbour (b). **35 ASCALON STUDIOS, inc.:** David Ascalon (r). **36 Alamy Stock Photo:** United Archives GmbH (cl). **36-37 Alamy Stock Photo:** dpa picture alliance (c). **37 Alamy Stock Photo:** BRIAN HARRIS (cr). **Getty Images:** Hulton Archive (cra); Science & Society Picture Library (cla). **38-39 Alamy Stock Photo:** Lordprice Collection. **39 akg-images:** Interfoto (tr). **Dorling Kindersley:** By kind permission of The Trustees of the Imperial War Museum, London (c); Wardrobe Museum, Salisbury (br). **40 Dorling Kindersley:** Eden Camp Museum (bc). **41 Alamy Stock Photo:** Stocktrek Images, Inc (bc). **Getty Images:** Maeers (cb); ullstein bild (t). **Mary Evans Picture Library:** Sueddeutsche Zeitung Photo (ca). **42-43 Getty Images:** Time Life Pictures. **43 Imperial War Museum:** (cra/ helmet). **iStockphoto.com:** Tropicalpixsingapore (crb). **Warbird Depot:** Doug Fisher (cra). **44 Alamy Stock Photo:** LH Images (tc); Art Directors & TRIP (cla). **45 Dorling Kindersley:** Eden Camp Museum (c). **Getty Images:** The National Archives (tc). **46 Dorling Kindersley:** Imperial War Museum, London (l). **Getty Images:** Bletchley Park Trust (crb). **47 Alamy Stock Photo:** Louis Berk (t); INTERFOTO (crb). **Getty Images:** Bletchley Park Trust (bc). **48-49 Alamy Stock Photo:** Martin Bennett (b). **Getty Images:** John Parrot / Stocktrek Images (t). **50 Dorling Kindersley:** Eden Camp Museum, Yorkshire (All). **51 Alamy Stock Photo:** INTERFOTO. **52 Dorling Kindersley:** RAF Museum, Cosford (ca). **Rex Shutterstock:** Peter Carroll / AP (clb). **53 Alamy Stock Photo:** Peter Horree (tl); Vahan Nersesyan (tr). **Getty Images:** Picture Post (br); George Silk / The LIFE Picture Collection (bl). **54 Alamy Stock Photo:** Photo Researchers, Inc (cl); World History Archive (c/background). **Dorling Kindersley:** Bradbury Science Museum, Los Alamos (c). **Library of Congress, Washington, D.C.:** (tl). **54-55 Alamy Stock Photo:** World History Archive (t). **Getty Images:** Bernard Hoffman (b). **55 123RF.com:** Katawuth Yupparach (crb). **Getty Images:** Keystone (cr). **56 Getty Images:** Hulton Deutsch (cl); Fox Photos (cr); Keystone Features (cb). **57 Getty Images:** Heritage Images (clb); Universal History Archive (cla); Underwood Archives (cra). **Rex Shutterstock:** Creativ Studio Heinemann / imageBROKER (crb). **58 Dorling Kindersley:** RAF Museum, Cosford (cra). **Getty Images:** ullstein bild (ca). **iStockphoto.com:** Daboost (clb); KeithBishop (tr). **59 iStockphoto. com:** Ilyabolotov (cl). **59 iStockphoto. com:** Daboost (clb); KeithBishop (tl); Jeremy (cl); Olga Mallari (clb); lightkitegirl (bc/all); Macrovector (br/all). **60 Dorling Kindersley:** Eden Camp Museum (bc). **Getty Images:** Historical (tl). **61 Dorling Kindersley:** The Tank Museum (tr). **62 bnps.co.uk:** Laura Jones (tl). **64 123RF. com:** Scott Fensome / zollster (tl)

Cover images: Front: **Alamy Stock Photo:** Martin Bennett br, Art Directors & TRIP ca, INTERFOTO fcrb; **Dorling Kindersley:** Tony Corbin / War and Peace Show l, Eden Camp Museum cr, Royal Airforce Museum, London cra/ (plane), Wardrobe Museum, Salisbury cra, Wardrobe Museum, Salisbury tr; **Getty Images:** John Parrot / Stocktrek Images crb; Back: **Dorling Kindersley:** University of Aberdeen cr, Gatwick Aviation Museum tr; **Getty Images:** SVF2 bl; Spine: **Dorling Kindersley:** Wardrobe Museum, Salisbury c; Front Flap: **Dorling Kindersley:** Eden Camp Museum, Yorkshire cla, cra, RAF Museum, Cosford br, RAF Museum, Cosford tr/ (plane), Wardrobe Museum, Salisbury clb, Wardrobe Museum, Salisbury cr; **Rex Shutterstock:** AP bc; Back Flap: **Alamy Stock Photo:** Ian Macpherson London cr; **Dorling Kindersley:** University of Aberdeen crb, Scale Model World, Allan Toyne b; Front Endpapers: **Alamy Stock Photo:** akg-images 0tc, Peter Horree 0tr, PF-(aircraft) 0crb; **Dorling Kindersley:** Bradbury Science Museum, Los Alamos 0ftr, RAF Museum, Cosford 0cla, Royal Airforce Museum, London 0cla (Hawker), The Tank Museum 0ca; **Getty Images:** Bentley Archive / Popperfoto 0fbr, Keystone-France 0ca (bentino), Historical 0clb, Stocktrek Images 0fbl, Universal History Archive 0ftl, 0bc, 0cb.

All other images © Dorling Kindersley
For further information see: www.dkimages.com